JUST THE FACTS: ON RESEARCHING YOUR NONFICTION CHILDREN'S BOOK

LISA L. OWENS

THE-EFA.ORG

Copyright © 2020 by Lisa L. Owens
Cover and design © 2020 Editorial Freelancers Association
New York, NY

All rights reserved.
No part of this publication may be reproduced, distributed, or transmitted in any form or by any means, including, but not limited to, photocopying, recording, or other electronic or mechanical methods, without the prior written permission of the publisher, except in the case of brief quotations embodied in critical reviews and certain other noncommercial uses permitted by copyright law. For permission requests, write to the publisher at "Attention: Publications Chairperson," at the address below.

266 West 37th St. 20th Floor
New York, NY 10018
office@the-efa.org

ISBN paperback   978-1-880407-33-2
ISBN ebook   978-1-880407-34-9

Published in the United States of America by the Editorial Freelancers Association.
Subject Categories: **LANGUAGE ARTS & DISCIPLINES** | Authorship | Writing | Nonfiction | Children's & Young Adult | **REFERENCE** / Research

Legal Disclaimer
While the publisher and author have made every attempt to verify that the information provided in this book is correct and up to date, the publisher and author assume no responsibility for any error, inaccuracy, or omission.

The advice, examples, and strategies contained herein are not suitable for every situation. Neither the publisher nor author shall be liable for damages arising therefrom. This book is not intended for use as a source of legal or financial advice. Running a business involves complex legal and financial issues. You should always retain competent legal and financial professionals to provide guidance.

EFA Publications Director: Robin Martin
Copyeditor: Billy Lombardo
Proofreader: Jared Carew
Book Designer: Kevin Callahan | BNGO Books
Cover Designer: Ann Marie Manca

Owens, Lisa L.
Author site: llowens.com
Editorial services site: owenseditorialink.com
LinkedIn profile: linkedin.com/in/lisalowens/
Blog: llowens.blogspot.com
Twitter: @LisaLOwens
Instagram: @llowriter

To facts.
May they always matter.

And to young fans of nonfiction.
May we kidlit creators always do right by them.

Contents

Foreword	vii
PART I Wading In	1
PART II Digging In	7
PART III Getting (and Vetting) the Goods	15
APPENDIX A Select Projects and Their Sources	23
APPENDIX B Terms to Know	25
APPENDIX C Recommended Resources	27
About the Author	31
About the Editorial Freelancers Association (EFA)	32

Foreword

Have you heard? Nonfiction for children is having a moment. Young readers devour it and want more. Schools use it in the classroom. Some adult readers turn to it when they want to learn something new in a more digestible form — and also because there are so many outstanding books in this category. Nonfiction styles are evolving, and publishers are not only seeking the next big thing, but they're also looking for freshly presented evergreen topics.

It's an exciting time for writers, whether you've been working in the nonfiction realm for a while or this is a new-to-you writerly pursuit. Either way, there's room for your voice and perspective. Someone, somewhere is waiting to take a bite out of your slice-of-life picture book biography of an unexpected figure; to discover your innovative "way in" to exploring a science topic; to burn through your inspirational graphic memoir; or to learn a valuable life skill from your offbeat how-to. By all means, write that book! Just be sure to proceed with the understanding that the research behind any nonfiction work must hold up under intense scrutiny.

Children's books are short and easy to read. How hard can they be to research and write? Right?

Be honest. This thought, or fervent hope, has crossed your mind at one time or another, and that's okay; we all start from the beginning and learn as we go. But seasoned pros will tell you that while a good children's book may appear simple, achieving that impression requires the dedicated practice of a complex writing craft. And the research that informs works for children should follow the same standards used for adult-market publications. The truth, as best we know it, is always paramount.

The nonfiction writer's job is to craft an engaging and enlightening book supported by the most credible source material available. Now, *of course* a book's narrative, structure, and format are key. We all strive to create something that entices kids to pick up the book . . . followed by that next book, too.

But writing to the "non" in nonfiction takes more procedural and creative effort than you might think, and relatively few of us start out with a proper inkling of what that effort can entail—or how it will change from project to project. Which brings me to the purpose of this concise guide. The "why" of my narrow focus on research alone.

As an editor, I've seen too many nicely written nonfiction manuscripts fall apart once the facts within are evaluated during the publishing process. I can think of only a few cases in which writers have knowingly included faulty or misleading information. Such behavior is rare. More often than not, glitches occur when well-meaning authors simply don't yet know what they don't know about conducting solid research. That is a fixable problem, and I want to help!

My goal is to offer up my favorite go-to strategies for finding, sourcing, and vetting *just the facts* you need to help shape any kidlit nonfiction project in your mind's eye. Advice and tips stem from my own decades of experience writing and editing children's nonfiction, and I hope you will be able to grab some plum insights and to-dos/to-tries to add to your own process.

The Core Topic at a Glance

Today's successful children's nonfiction author must

- believe that facts matter
- embrace the crucial role research plays in any project, no matter its audience or length
- know the difference between cursory and quality research
- model good research practices for young readers
- tap into the joy of chasing new knowledge, and in sharing it with others
- bring all of the above to bear on each new book

Just the Facts: Researching Your Nonfiction Children's Book

> *A 10-year-old knows a lot.*
> *If you think she or he isn't noticing the world*
> *around them, you're missing a lot.*
> — Jacqueline Woodson

As You Read: A Suggested Exercise

The sample project plan you'll find in this booklet includes creating a dedicated notebook for each new nonfiction project; I recommend creating that notebook now, assuming you haven't already done so.

To help reinforce this booklet's lessons, you can use the notebook to keep a running dialogue with yourself about how this discussion applies to your own work. Maybe you'd like to improve your current work in progress (WIP), or figure out what to write, or what to write next, or even how to start your nonfiction writer's journey from scratch.

Take notes along the way to underscore any advice you'd like to incorporate into your routine. Start a project-specific to-do list. Brainstorm topics and titles. Write down your dream-big writing goals.

The simple act of putting pen to paper in this intentional way can help build excitement and solidify your commitment to what's next for you. And I think it can bring home a guiding principle of this work: that your nonfiction project research, as well as your professional-development research, is always consciously or unconsciously in process. It's part of the fabric of your writing life and involves so much more than finding facts in a book or googling key words.

PART I

Wading In

*A writer has the duty to be good, not lousy;
true, not false; lively, not dull;
accurate, not full of error.*
—E. B. White

Let's start by establishing what research means in this discussion.

As part of the nonfiction-writing process, I define *research* as a systematic investigation of any topic, character, setting, narrative, and format details needed to inform the writing.

Any investigation must be thorough and conducted with integrity. Sometimes you will have ample time to chase down research, but be aware that if you're working to a contracted professional deadline, the schedule will at some point dictate how much research you can realistically do.

> Research *is a systematic investigation of any topic, character, setting, narrative, and format details needed to inform the writing of a given nonfiction project.*

Research As Serious Fun

If research is starting to sound dull right about now, hang on! I invite you to reflect on and lean in to its many charms. One way or another, research has been part of your life. You've done it for school. For work and play and health and safety, for anything and everything you've felt called to learn. You know you've disappeared down the rabbit hole while purposefully chasing a detail, and you have loved it.

When I'm writing a book whose premise fascinates me, the research feels like treasure hunting, even (or perhaps especially) when the hunting gets tough. There's nothing quite like stepping on the needle in a haystack you actually set out to find. Having an incredible factoid land in your lap seemingly out of the blue is just as thrilling.

Because you are pursuing the craft of nonfiction writing, chances are good that you're no stranger to curiosity. You're obviously curious about your subject matter, and possibly even about any person, place, thing, or life situation that turns your head.

Curiosity is key to being a writer, no matter what you create. As a nonfiction specialist, you must know your topic well enough to write with authority. And that authority grows as you write. You will want to leave room enough in your process to allow the writing itself to help you synthesize and improve your research.

The research-writing-research-writing cycle continues throughout the life of any project. Staying curious keeps you going as you question what you're reading, and as you seek information and confirmation. Curiosity keeps your writer's brain percolating in the background while you turn your attention to other things, and it produces the occasional "A-ha!" lightning bolt that clarifies what your book is about—or what it *should* be about.

This quote from author Zora Neale Hurston speaks to the heart of my research philosophy: "Research is formalized curiosity. It is poking and prodding with a purpose."

All that purposeful, ever-curious attention to detail makes it possible to craft a book that successfully conveys the work's point to its readers. Research helps you identify concrete goals and provides a solid foundation for writing relatable, authentic prose that readers will connect with and trust as factual.

> *"Research is formalized curiosity.
> It is poking and prodding
> with a purpose."*
> — Zora Neale Hurston

Reflection Exercise

Take a moment to remember a recent bout with intense curiosity. Something that made you stop what you were doing to learn more. What did that kind of curiosity feel like? Were you able to satisfy it? If so, how?

Now think about your nonfiction work in progress (WIP). It's fine if it's still in the idea phase. Recall coming up with your idea and how you felt at the time. Is your interest in the topic still strong? Are you itching to learn more? Why or why not?

As with any reflection exercise, there are no wrong answers. Just an opportunity to check in with yourself and use what you learn for whatever it's worth.

An Insider's Aside
In the interest of keeping it real, I'll admit to having written about a few topics I didn't readily connect with.

Before finding a home in children's publishing, I was an investigative reporter for arts-and-entertainment weeklies. I pitched my own story ideas, but occasionally I'd receive mandatory assignments. If a topic didn't draw me in, I had to find a way to fire up my interest. Research helped. Conducting interviews, reading documents, sitting in on meetings, and so on, would inevitably reveal enough facts to ignite *my* best story angle, and I'd be off to the races.

As a children's author, I've run into a similar issue with a few write for hire (WFH) books whose concepts were set before I signed on to write them. Going through the motions as a disinterested writer is no fun, and I will do everything within my power to ensure that I find a way to enjoy my work. And in this writing realm, too, research has come to my rescue.

While noticing cool details and promising anecdotes during preliminary inquiries, it's easy to discover what I want to know more about. And I ask: How can I approach the required topic with my interests embedded in the framework? Could I, for example, start a scientific exploration with that controversial position and work backward or forward to arrive at today's accepted conclusion? Or, in a biography, could I lead with an episode from the subject's colorful childhood that mind-blowingly foreshadows important future events in her life?

What I know for sure is that intentionally finding the angle most interesting to me is what makes that story "mine" to tell. And consequently, it lends a natural enthusiasm and authenticity to my authorial voice—invisible qualities readers naturally respond to.

The Dual Role of Writer-Researcher

Keep in mind that as your concept's originator and primary advocate, it is up to you to create your investigation's scope and process. This holds true whether you're publishing in the traditional market or doing WFH work for the school-and-library market. Nobody can, or will, plan the research for you.

Also, as an author, YOU decide what your book is *really* about and you execute your vision for how to structure your text, and in what format you'd like the whole work presented.

Yes, your publisher will weigh in with feedback ranging from opinions and suggestions to full-stop revision requirements. And, yes, sometimes after you've firmly decided what you're writing, you will change course on your own when the deep research and writing work you're doing shows you a better way. That's how the best outcomes come about.

Here are some theoretical decisions you might weigh while determining what your book *is*, using biography as an example:

Just the Facts: Researching Your Nonfiction Children's Book

- Should you write the person's cradle-to-grave story, explore a particular era, or focus on just one defining event from the character's life?
- Does your chosen angle work best as a picture book for younger readers or a book meant for more sophisticated young adults? Maybe something else in-between?
- Will you write using spare lyrical prose or fashion an exciting narrative adventure?
- Do you want the book to be traditionally illustrated or photo-illustrated? Or might the content lend itself to being presented in a unique format, such as a pop-up book, a graphic biography, or an illustrated timeline filled with milestones and quotes?

Now is a good time to consider: *Are you familiar enough with the children's nonfiction landscape to start making real decisions about your project?*

Even if the answer is a firm yes, you understand that market research can enhance your project plan and that the publishing landscape is ever evolving. You will still want to check out other nonfiction books on your topic to see how your desired concept, style, and format compare. That intel could reinforce your instincts, inspire you to tweak one element, completely shift gears, or cause you to shelve your idea for the time being or forever.

Not to worry if you don't yet feel well grounded in children's nonfiction. Luckily, it's easy to begin your learning quest.

As a first step, I suggest studying online listings of award-winning children's nonfiction, reviews, relevant book blogs, best-of lists by industry organizations and publications, and recommended reading lists created by libraries and booksellers. You'll be exposed to a wide variety of recent nonfiction while developing your ability to spot, and emulate, the cream of the crop.

Next, begin what will become a career-long practice: haunting your local libraries and bookstores.

Reading widely is an essential part of the writing life. So is connecting with librarians and booksellers who can help you find resources to feed the research beast of any given project. Turn to them for assistance finding

- books with obscure subject matter or innovative formats
- super-specific details that you think and hope exist but can't locate
- mentor texts marked by the quality and integrity you'd like to emulate
- the hottest or most-respected titles that might compare to or compete with the book you're hoping to create

RESEARCH, all!

PART II
Digging In

Now that you're more comfortable with the idea of researching your book, it's time to dig in and do it.

This will come as no surprise, but it needs to be said: Every book requires its own type and amount of research. Although you should bank on fulfilling standard broad-stroke requirements, there is no one-size-fits-all plan.

> *Every book requires its own type and amount of research.*

Where to Start

You may have learned the Five Ws and One H (5W1H) in school. These shorthand questions—Who? What? When? Where? Why? How?—are widely used in journalistic and other types of investigations.

Notice that none of them can be answered with yes or no, and that's by design. Replies to open-ended questions like "What happened?" for example, naturally paint a fuller picture than a closed question like "Did an earthquake happen?"

Finding the factual answers to open-ended questions helps a children's nonfiction author gather the most basic information needed to frame a story, along with richer details about elements such as:

- personal character traits
- a setting's physical and geographical features
- historical, social, and cultural context
- EVERYTHING, when you get right down to it

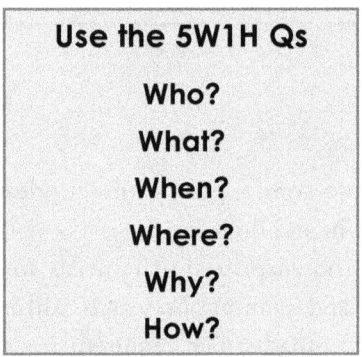

Sample Project Plan

Research and writing go hand in glove. You can't write children's nonfiction without doing your research. But as important as research is, an author must prioritize job one: the writing.

Your best bet when starting a new book project is to envision your ideal scenario—what the book will be, how you will accomplish that result—and create a plan for reaching milestone goals. Start where you are with the information you have and sketch it out. You will update the plan down the road as the writing comes along and other circumstances unfold.

Here is a typical early-stage process I use once I've committed to a new book idea.

> *Writing nonfiction is more like sculpture,*
> *a matter of shaping the research*
> *into the finished thing.*
> —Joan Didion

Complete a round of 5W1H.

- I can't formulate a meaningful plan without that topic information in hand. I want to know enough to be able to envision an approach to writing the book.

Grab a fresh notebook.

- I designate one notebook per project for note-taking on the go, brainstorming, testing ideas, and drafting short passages.

Begin identifying and collecting source material.

- I check my own physical and digital libraries and round up relevant resources, including books, ebooks, audiobooks, DVDs, and documentaries housed on streaming services. I search for good online resources. Then I place library holds and pick them up in batches, visiting the stacks to look for more books. If I think I need to interview experts or subjects, or to visit museums, special collections, or locations that serve as primary sources, I list those.
- I like to build a preliminary materials collection and figure out which sources stay and go later. This process continues through the life of a project.

Start writing.

- I usually have enough information from 5W1H to attempt some freewriting. I might try out different opening lines, write up a short scene I feel confident about, or play with a writing style.
- It's anybody's guess whether any of this early writing will appear in the final manuscript. But this is the time to get my writing juices flowing. Writing begets writing. And the forward motion helps me start working out the appropriate voice and tone for the book and feel assured that a WIP is truly *in progress*.
- **A caveat about personal writing styles:** You absolutely can start writing the minute a new topic idea pops into your head. If that's your style, run with it. You do you!

Outline the book.

- I work better with a roadmap in place, so before going too far down any writing path, I outline. And I keep it simple. The outline created for my project-planning purposes is for my eyes only. Outlines I might provide the publisher during an active project or send with an editor or agent nonfiction proposal belong in a different discussion. I use my outline as both a plan and a check on its logical structure and completeness.
- This guide's table of contents, for example, was my outline. It's pretty spare. But because I've lived this information and often presented it in workshop formats, I didn't need a detailed roadmap. Did it change as I wrote? Constantly! Any outline will, regardless of your familiarity with the topic.
- My outline for the narrative chapter book *Women Pilots of World War II* included a short description of each element in the book, including chapters, sidebars, and back matter.
- Note that my outlining process for any book includes creating descriptive section and/or chapter titles to use as signposts for the major landmarks I want to hit along my path. I refine these as I write (another take on the writing as research!). This exercise, in particular, helps me see whether and when I've hit upon a logical structure that fits my vision.

Create a system for organizing findings.

- My office space is well used. On the desk and the shelf behind my desk (and even next to my favorite living room chair), I set up curated stacks of any physical resources I own. I also keep bags of library books handy, either in my office or just outside the door. My high-tech bagging system keeps the library books from getting misplaced.
- If I've interviewed sources, I keep any recordings and transcriptions in the project's Dropbox folder, and the same goes for any photo research I've compiled (always properly labeled with source material stored).
- These days I use file drawers strictly for archived items, so any project-specific papers I might want to shuffle reside on my desk, within reach.

- To capture online sources for review, I use Google Bookmarks and private YouTube playlists. For one WIP, I saved an unseemly number of Twitter bookmarks that I finally exported to a spreadsheet. I don't recommend that approach if you, as I did at the time while actively writing *other* books, think it's a good idea to save Twitter bookmarks for the better part of a year without regularly going back to cull them.
- When writing in Scrivener, which I occasionally do, I like to use its research-collection feature. And recently, while working on longer-form YA nonfiction, I've come to love and rely on the reference manager Zotero for creating citations and storing links to online sources.
- My system may seem involved as described, but it's pretty tidy in practice and works for me. Your system, once you find it, will work for you.

Work up a writing schedule.

- When I'm working on a WFH book, that timeline is set by the publisher. Simply adding the project deadlines to my calendar usually suffices. But if I'm writing on spec, I set personal deadline goals. I'll assign a due date for the first draft and work backward to fill in milestones I'd like to hit along the way. Depending on the length of a project and whatever else is going on in my world, milestones could include daily word-count or weekly chapter-count goals.
- The key is to set realistic goals that keep me on task and moving forward. Because I've had tons of practice writing to schedule, I generally have a good handle on what I can and *can't* accomplish in a given time frame. My writing-muscle memory is strong. But then again . . . life happens and plans will sometimes change.

The key is to set realistic goals to keep yourself on task and your writing moving forward.

Learn more about the topic than can be explored in the book, but resist the urge to research forever.

- Most nonfiction writers I know would agree that research is fun. It's easy to keep working those search engines and burning through your book stacks. Just don't fall into the trap of thinking you can't write your book until you know all the things.
- Your research shows you which facts should be expressly included in the story you're telling and which ones should live in the background. It also gives you the confidence to authoritatively write to plan. At some point, you will know exactly what your book is about and when you have enough research to support its content. Above all else, you must keep up with your writing.

Keep writing and researching. Rinse and repeat.

- As you write, the big-picture holes in your content and the narrower, more specific details you need to locate will continually reveal themselves. Think about how narratives unfold for you as you're reading. You know and don't know what comes next until all becomes clear. Then take to heart the knowledge that the same thing happens while writing, except that you're driving the bus while paving your way to a new destination.
- The narrative you're crafting in your manuscript doesn't just present itself for you to type out. You have to work it out on the page. Your book will show you what you need to know as it takes shape and gets stronger.

Your book will show you what you need to know as it takes shape and gets stronger.

Finish your draft.

- That's it. That's the step.

Give it a rest.

- Step away from your manuscript and revisit it later with a fresh, objective eye.
- If you've let the manuscript marinate long enough, you're in for some surprises. Though the work is familiar, it may feel like another writer hijacked your document to add a few seriously good passages, as well as a few glaringly bad bits.
- You will spot holes in logic, maybe even misstatements or factual characterizations that could be misconstrued if not restated. And you will be ready to fully appreciate your accomplishment and look forward to taking the book to its next, better level.

Set new research and revision goals.

- You are well on your way now. Keep going!

PART III
Getting (and Vetting) the Goods

You've chosen a topic, created a research plan, and started the writing. Great! You're on solid footing. Which means you can take a breather to more fully explore a variety of potential research tools without losing your writing mojo.

It's easy to suffer from tunnel vision while in the thick of the writing, and that can lead to a convenient reliance on only the most obvious resources, such as books, articles, and the top five online search results. I hope the following roundups, or touchstone lists, can serve as memory joggers and idea sparkers.

Tools and Tips

Potential sources are all around you; perhaps not for the specific thing you're researching in the moment, but under the right circumstances, anything can be source material. It's important to keep an open mind and think outside the typical research box, especially at the beginning of your process and during times you feel stuck. Taking a moment to imagine new sourcing avenues can help loosen your grip on what you already have found and reignite your creativity.

In the meantime, this tried-and-true toolkit will help you cover a great deal of fact-finding ground. An "and so on" for each bullet point is implied.

- **Media:** books, newspapers, magazines, music, documents, directories, letters, maps, films, photographs, artwork, ads
- **Life experience:** childhood, school and work, travel, relationships, events, lessons learned, cultural customs, hobbies, interests
- **Live subjects:** people, animals, places, objects, artifacts
- **The internet:** online everything

When considering research tools, it's important to keep an open mind and think outside the box.

PRO TIP: Be sure to carefully track your sources from the start. Know which ones you've used and which facts they informed in your manuscript. Many children's nonfiction publishers will require you to provide sourcing information. Some of it may get listed in your bibliography and other back matter. And you could be asked to submit photocopies or scans showing the facts as presented in your sources. Even if a publisher doesn't ask to see this information, you should keep it on file anyway. You'll need to refer to it during the editorial process if any questions come up—and you would be wise to hang on to it for some time in case any (extremely rare) post-publication issues with the content arise.

Be Worldly and Think Locally

The communication paths and fingertip access to research nonfiction writers have is nothing short of amazing. We can connect with experts and databases located around the world. Just think about that for a second!

You should make use of internet and other digital resources, but don't forget to think locally with regard to any in-person research you might conduct. "Locally" can mean local to you or your subject matter.

For example, in researching a book set in nineteenth-century Iowa—where I don't live—thinking locally meant seeking information found in Iowa. My inquiry led me to primary-source writings at the Iowa State Historical Society and artifacts in University of Iowa Libraries Special Collections. My research also included onsite visits to relevant towns and structures, as well as interviews with locals who had knowledge of my subject matter.

Thinking locally *to me* while researching the same project from my Pacific Northwest–based home entailed connecting with nearby experts who taught me something new related to the history or who were qualified to vet the accuracy of my writing.

PRO TIP: If you are reluctant to ask individual experts or entities to answer a few questions or point you toward resources, don't be. Most will be only too happy to hear from you. Just be polite and respectful of their time. You don't want to overstep. And if you request expert feedback on your work, know that you should offer payment.

Random Local Sources of Inspiration

telephone directories	cemeteries	service organizations
colleges and universities	charitable organizations	major businesses and factories
local newspapers	zoos and wildlife preserves	historic registries
antiques shops	yearbooks	Chambers of Commerce
art installations	parks and beaches	government offices
community newsletters	regional magazines	clubs and associations
teachers and scholars	places of worship	musicians and sports figures
cultural centers	schools and hospitals	artisans and scientists
military outfits	agricultural centers	state fair exhibits
small business owners	animal shelters	police and fire departments
government officials	community leaders	political figures

Top-Tier Research Websites to Check Out

These are some of my all-time favorite online repositories of high-quality information.

Some sites require registration and/or a subscription fee in order to access their records. Others are either completely free or offer free versions granting more limited access to their collection. All are worth exploring and keeping on your radar.

PRO TIP: If a subscription-based site looks like a great resource for your project, it's worth finding out if it offers a free trial period. If so, and with a good plan of attack, you can access materials during the limited time frame, making sure to cancel before the trial is up. And don't forget to check with your library. It may offer patrons free access to certain subscriptions.

- academia.edu: academic papers
- ancestry.com: birth, death, marriage, census, military, immigration, family history, records
- archives.gov: government docs, military records, geographic/biographic histories
- gettyimages.com: archival historical-image research
- gutenberg.org: Project Gutenberg database of 60K ebooks in the public domain
- jstor.org: journals, primary sources, books
- loc.gov: Library of Congress digital library, image and audio collections, educator resources, research and reference services
- nasa.gov: all things space from a network of NASA sites
- newspaperarchive.com: online newspaper archive
- newspapers.com: online newspaper archive
- publishersmarketplace.com: market news and book deals
- scholar.google.com: Google Scholar search engine specific to scholarly literature
- siarchives.si.edu: Smithsonian Institution Archives

Consider the Source

Now that you've been gathering information, how do you determine whether a given fact is *good*? Well, you'll want to take first things first, and the first step is to consider the source.

Primary vs. Secondary

Primary-source materials are the gold standard for nonfiction writing. A primary source is an original document or artifact offering firsthand information about an event from the event's time. Use as many of them as you can.

For example, a letter written by Abraham Lincoln during the Civil War is a primary source. A twenty-first century article discussing Lincoln's state of mind while writing that letter relies on the letter as its primary source. But the article itself is a secondary source because it interprets the original letter.

Most writers rely on a mix of primary and secondary sources.

> *A primary source is an original document or artifact offering firsthand information about a person or event. Examples are newspapers of the time, journals, photographs, oral histories, memoirs, data, speeches, and government documents.*

> *A secondary source uses primary sources to interpret or analyze an event after the fact. Examples include journal articles, books, and reviews.*

The Rule of Three

For any fact included in your work, best-practice process dictates following the rule of three, or securing at least three credible sources to support each fact. Publishers I work with adhere to that rule, making occasional exceptions to accept just two backup sources.

PRO TIP: Children's nonfiction publishers do not accept children's books, Wikipedia, blogs, or op-eds as sources to support your facts. Note that all of those can point you toward acceptable sources, so do check them for quality leads.

Testing, Testing

Before turning in the manuscript, you should take the opportunity to thoroughly test your research. I use these questions and considerations to evaluate the strength of each fact. If I already know the answers in relation to most of the facts at this stage, I concentrate on finding any straggler facts in the book I have not fully vetted.

- **Who is the author or speaker of the fact? Are they viewed as legitimate?** I consider credentials, experience, status, track record, and any known biases.
- **Did the source's author cite sources?** If yes, what percentage of them are primary, and can I spot-check any of them? If not, why not?
- **What is the credibility of the source's publisher?** Do I already know, or can I find out?
- **Did I find at least two, and preferably three, corroborating sources for each factual assertion in my book?** If no, can I find additional sources now? Or might I need to edit out or recast certain assertions?
- **When was the fact last "settled" according to my findings?** If it was fifty years ago, did I check that it's not in dispute again now?
- **Does a snippet from the source content I used pass the search engine test?** Sometimes I find many books on the same topic that seem to quote each other. So when I notice a strong similarity among passages, I type part of the text into a search engine and see if I get near-exact or exact hits. If I do, I'll want to investigate further and make changes. I might substitute a different quote or eliminate a fact that I just can't support.

Having made sure you've checked on every fact in your book and made necessary adjustments, you can now take a bit of a breather and a low bow. You've reached a huge milestone. Well done!

Just the Facts: Researching Your Nonfiction Children's Book

For argument's sake, we'll assume that soon the book will find its way to your editor's desk and begin the next leg of its publication journey.

The writing and the research will be put under the microscope at this stage, possibly by the editor, an expert reviewer, and a fact-checker or a copyeditor who performs fact-checking.

But you are not worried. You are ready to share your sources and methods, handle any challenges to your work, and get your book into the hands of readers so they can delight in *just the facts* and so much more.

APPENDIX A
Select Projects and Their Sources

Books by Lisa L. Owens	Sample Sources
American Justice: Seven Famous Trials of the 20th Century High-interest narrative nonfiction for reluctant middle grade to YA readers.	court transcripts, published interviews with key figures, courtroom footage, legal briefs, government reports, photo archives, TV news coverage, newspaper articles, adult nonfiction
Bigfoot: The Legend Lives On Informational fiction chapter book for upper-elementary to middle grade readers.	academic expert interview, Bigfoot enthusiasts' discussion list, documentaries, adult nonfiction, newspaper articles, cultural mythology
Frenemies: *Dealing with Friend Drama* Self-help book for tween–teen girls featuring fictional conflict scenarios, discussion questions, author commentary, and a psychologist's advice (ghost-written by the author) for resolving conflict.	research on relational and other social-emotional learning issues, the author's teenage diaries, magazines for teen girls, psychologist's media platform/writing voice/clinical philosophies

Go to School Title in an informational picture book series introducing social groups to ages 4–8.	teacher interviews, elementary curriculum info, classroom setups and school layouts, staff lists w/roles delineated
Heroes of Dunkirk Narrative nonfiction chapter book for ages 8–10.	maps, WWII battle strategies and progression, archived radio broadcasts, official military records, declassified intelligence, survivor interviews on tape, modern podcast, adult nonfiction
A Journey with Hernán Cortés Biography for ages 8–10 created using only primary sources.	personal correspondence, maps, boat drawings, paintings, calendars, cultural artifacts, autobiographies
Neptune Title in a 10-title photo-illustrated informational picture book series about the solar system.	NASA's live feeds and missions histories, planetary news notifications, scholarly articles, news articles, satellite footage, in-depth photo research, astronomer biographies
Pilgrims in America Middle-grade narrative nonfiction.	diaries, letters, artifacts, scholarly literature, academic expert interview

APPENDIX B
Terms to Know

back matter: parts of a book that appear in back, after the main text

bibliography: list of books the author consulted and/or referred to in the book's text

browsable nonfiction: entertaining facts presented in short bites within an eye-catching format

citation: reference to a source

ebook: digital book

expository nonfiction: text meant to inform the reader about its topic using a standard organizing structure such as description, chronology, compare and contrast, cause and effect, or how-to

freewriting: practice of writing freely, without care, for a period of time

graphic memoir: autobiographical story told in graphic novel/comics format

informational fiction: narrative that deliberately features both factual and fictional elements

kidlit: term for children's literature commonly used in the industry

narrative nonfiction: nonfiction that presents informational material using an engaging storytelling structure

on spec: writing on spec means to produce work without a contract in place

primary source: original document or artifact offering firsthand information about an event or person

proposal: pitch used to sell a nonfiction book to a publisher; children's authors often submit a nonfiction proposal before writing the full manuscript

public domain: work that isn't protected by intellectual property laws

secondary source: source that interprets or analyzes an event after the fact

STEM: acronym for an educational curriculum combining science, technology, engineering, and math. Variations include STEAM, with the addition of art; and STREAM with the addition of wRiting.

Scrivener: word-processing and outlining program designed for authors

submission: piece of writing sent to an agent or editor for their consideration

tone: expression of attitude through writing

voice: quality of an author's style that makes their writing unique

APPENDIX C
Recommended Resources

Blogs

The Brown Bookshelf: news, reviews, and interviews raising awareness of African American voices writing for young readers
thebrownbookshelf.com/

Celebrate Science: nonfiction writing tips, resources for science teachers
celebratescience.blogspot.com/

A Fuse #8 Production: book reviews
http://blogs.slj.com/afuse8production/

From the Mixed-Up Files of Middle-Grade Authors: booklists, author interviews, market news
romthemixedupfiles.com/

Literary Rambles: interviews with literary agents, posts by kidlit creators
literaryrambles.com/

Manuscript Wish List: wished-for books posted by agents and editors
manuscriptwishlist.com/

Nerdy Book Club: booklists, reviews, creator interviews
nerdybookclub.wordpress.com/

The Nonfiction Detectives (archived): book reviews
nonfictiondetectives.com/

We Need Diverse Books: blog and other resources promoting literature that reflects the lives of all young people
diversebooks.org/

Children's Nonfiction Awards

Bank Street College of Education Best Children's Books of the Year

Boston Globe-Horn Book Awards

Children's Book Guild Nonfiction Award

The Cybils Awards

Crystal Kite Awards

Excellence in Nonfiction

Giverny Award

Golden Kite Awards

Orbis Pictus Award for Outstanding Nonfiction

Robert F. Sibert Informational Book Medal

Mentor Texts

Best Friends by Shannon Hale, illustrated by LeUyen Pham (First Second, 2019): graphic memoir for ages 8–11

Bomb: The Race to Build—and Steal—the World's Most Dangerous Weapon by Steve Sheinkin (Flash Point, 2012): narrative nonfiction for ages 10–14

Emmanuel's Dream: The True Story of Emmanuel Ofosu Yeboah by Laurie Ann Thompson, illustrated by Sean Qualls (Schwartz & Wade, 2015): lyrical picture book biography for ages 4–8

Dazzle Ships: World War I and the Art of Confusion by Chris Barton, illustrated by Victo Ngai (Millbrook, 2017): narrative nonfiction picture book for ages 7–10

Just the Facts: Researching Your Nonfiction Children's Book

The Family Romanov: Murder, Rebellion, and the Fall of Imperial Russia by Candace Fleming (Schwartz & Wade, 2014): narrative nonfiction for ages 12 and up

Honeybee: The Busy Life of Apis Mellifera by Candace Fleming, illustrated by Eric Rohmann (Neal Porter Books, 2020): lyrical nonfiction picture book for ages 6–10

How They Croaked: The Awful Ends of the Awfully Famous by Georgia Bragg, illustrated by Kevin O'Malley (Bloomsbury Children's, 2012): browsable nonfiction for ages 10–14

Grand Canyon by Jason Chin (Roaring Book Press, 2017): expository nonfiction picture book for ages 7–12

Growing Up Gorilla: How a Zoo Baby Brought Her Family Together by Clare Hodgson Meeker (Millbrook Press, 2019): narrative nonfiction picture book for ages 8–12

Guts by Raina Telgemeier (Graphix, 2019): graphic memoir for ages 8–12

The Man Who Walked Between the Towers by Mordecai Gerstein: lyrical picture book biography for ages 5 and up

Pink Is for Blobfish by Jess Keating: expository nonfiction picture book for ages 5–8

Schomburg: The Man Who Built a Library by Carol Boston Weatherford, illustrated by Eric Velasquez: picture book biography for ages 8–12

Shout by Laurie Halse Anderson: free-verse memoir for ages 12 and up

13 1/2 Incredible Things You Need to Know About Everything (DK Children, 2017): browsable nonfiction for ages 8–12

The Undefeated by Kwame Alexander, illustrated by Kadir Nelson: poetic nonfiction picture book for ages 6–9

Unpresidented: A Biography of Donald Trump by Martha Brockenbrough: biography for ages 12–18

Professional Organizations

Authors Guild
Editorial Freelancers Association
National Association of Science Writers
Society of Children's Book Writers and Illustrators

Professional Publications

Ask
Booklist
Click
Cobblestone
Highlights
The Horn Book
Kirkus Reviews
Muse
National Geographic Kids
Publishers Weekly
School Library Journal

About the Author

Lisa L. Owens is the editor of hundreds of books for all ages and the author of 100+ children's titles. Her most recent nonfiction book, *Women Pilots of World War II* (Lerner, 2018), debuted at number one on Amazon's Hot New Releases in Children's Modern History. A long-time EFA member, Owens is a former Chapter Coordinator and Education Chairperson on the Board of Governors. Currently, she serves SCBWI Western Washington as its Nonfiction Coordinator. Visit llowens.com to learn more about her work or to inquire about hosting her for a school author talk or professional-development event.

About the
Editorial Freelancers Association (EFA)

Celebrating 50 Years!
Dedicated to the Education and Growth
of Editorial Freelancers

The EFA is a national not-for-profit — 501(c)6 — organization, headquartered in New York City, run by member volunteers, all of whom are also freelancers. The EFA's members, experienced in a wide range of professional skills, live and work all across the United States and in other countries.

A pioneer in organizing freelancers into a network for mutual support and advancement, the EFA is now recognized throughout the publishing industry as the source for professional editorial assistance.

We welcome people of every race, color, culture, religion or no religion, gender identity, gender expression, age, national or ethnic origin, ancestry, citizenship, education, ability, health, neurotype, marital/parental status, socio-economic background, sexual orientation, and/or military status. We are nothing without our members, and encourage everyone to volunteer and to participate in our community.

The EFA sells a variety of specialized booklets, not unlike this one, on topics of interest to editorial freelancers at the-efa.org.

The EFA hosts online, asynchronous courses, real-time webinars, and on-demand recorded webinars designed especially for freelance editors, writers, and other editorial specialists around the world. You can learn more about our Education Program at the-efa.org.

To learn about these and other EFA offerings, visit the-efa.org and join us on social media:

Twitter: @EFAFreelancers
Instagram: @efa_editors
Facebook: editorialfreelancersassociation
LinkedIn: editorial-freelancers

www.ingramcontent.com/pod-product-compliance
Lightning Source LLC
Chambersburg PA
CBHW071127030426
42336CB00013BA/2227